Scottish Slimmers
plain

contents

All values given in the recipes are for
calories, Checks and grams of fat (in that
order), excluding No-Check foods, and
are **per serving** unless stated otherwise.

lunch or brunch

one

12 blt pasta salad

45g/1½oz dry weight pasta twirls or 115g/4oz cooked
weight pasta twirls
1 tbsp low-calorie mayonnaise
Black pepper
2 rashers well trimmed, lean back bacon
4-5 cherry tomatoes
2 spring onions
Good handful of rocket leaves

1 If not already cooked, boil the pasta in lightly salted
boiling water until just tender. Drain, rinse under cold
water and drain thoroughly.

2 Mix the pasta with the low-calorie mayonnaise and
season with black pepper.

3 Grill the bacon, then chop roughly. Cut the tomatoes
in half and slice the spring onions.

4 Mix the bacon, tomatoes and spring onions into the
pasta. Toss the rocket leaves into the mixture and
serve.

4 x 200g potatoes
Spray oil
250g/9oz chestnut mushrooms
6-8 spring onions
150ml/5fl oz vegetable stock
1 tbsp tomato purée
Good pinch dried thyme
1 heaped tbsp finely chopped parsley
2 heaped tbsp reduced-fat Greek yoghurt
Black pepper

1 Microwave potatoes in their skins, on high approx. 20 minutes, or boil in their skins, until cooked through.

2 When cool enough to handle, cut in half lengthwise and scoop out centres leaving ½ cm/¼ inch layer of potato inside the skin. (Scooped out potato can be saved for another meal.) This can be prepared in advance.

3 Preheat oven to 220°C/gas mark 8.

4 Roughly chop mushrooms. Trim and slice spring onions.

5 Lightly spray insides and outsides of skins with oil. Place, cut-side down, on a baking sheet and bake 10 minutes. Turn skins over and bake another 10-15 minutes or until crisp and golden.

6 Meanwhile, spray a pan with oil and cook mushrooms and spring onions 3-4 minutes, stirring frequently until juices start to run. Stir in tomato purée and thyme. Stir in stock and simmer until liquid is reduced to about 2 tablespoons.

7 If skins are not yet ready, remove mushrooms from heat. When ready to serve, stir Greek yoghurt and parsley into mushrooms and heat through gently. Season with black pepper.

8 Remove skins from oven and spoon mushroom mixture into hollows. Serve 2 skins to each person.

one 240 **10** 17 red pepper, mushroom & cheese omelette

Spray oil
1 small onion, sliced
1 small red pepper (or half a large), sliced
3 mushrooms, sliced
2 medium eggs
30g/1oz half-fat cheddar, grated
No-Check salad to serve

1 Spray pan with oil and heat. Cook onions and peppers gently until softened. Add mushrooms and continue to cook a few minutes more until juices just start to run.

2 Beat the eggs and pour into the pan. Cook gently until set underneath.

3 Sprinkle with the grated cheese and flash under a pre-heated grill until top is lightly set and cheese has melted.

4 Serve omelette accompanied by No-Check salad.

ham & cottage cheese puff

1 medium egg
150g/5oz low-fat cottage cheese
30g/1oz lean ham, chopped
1 tbsp finely chopped parsley
Salt & black pepper

1 Pre-heat the oven to 200°C/gas mark 6.

2 Beat the egg in a bowl. Stir in the cottage cheese and mix well. Stir in the ham and parsley and season to taste.

3 Spray an ovenproof dish lightly with oil and pour in the cheese and ham mixture.

4 Bake in pre-heated oven approximately 20 minutes, or until puffed and golden.

four | 5 | vegetable rissoles

115g/4oz carrots, sliced
1 medium onion, roughly chopped
115g/4oz broccoli florets, roughly chopped
115g/4oz cauliflower, cabbage, courgettes or any other
No-Check vegetables.
85g/3oz sage & onion stuffing mix
1 large egg
1 tbsp seasoned flour for dipping rissoles
Spray oil

1 Cook vegetables in lightly salted boiling water until tender. Drain.

2 Put vegetables into a bowl, chop into small pieces and mix well. Add the dry stuffing mix. Leave until moisture in vegetables has soaked into stuffing mix and the mixture has become stiff.

3 Beat the egg, add to the vegetables and mix well.

4 Using a tablespoon, drop portions of the mixture into the seasoned flour to coat lightly. Shape into 8 flat round rissoles about 1 cm/½ inch thick.

5 Spray a non-stick pan with oil and heat. Fry rissoles 2-3 minutes on one side. Remove from pan and re-spray pan with oil. Cook the other side of the rissoles a further 2-3 minutes or until golden. Serve 2 rissoles to each person.

6 Could be served either with poached or dry-fried eggs, or some lean ham, or with baked beans. Or, with grilled tomatoes and either a jacket potato or some low-fat oven chips.

200g/7oz leeks
1 onion
900ml/1½ pints chicken or vegetable stock
60g/2oz instant potato powder
300ml/½ pint skimmed milk
Pepper to taste
Grated nutmeg
6 tbsp single cream
Freshly chopped chives to garnish

1 Trim, clean and chop leek and onion. Put into a pan together with the stock and bring to the boil. Reduce heat and simmer 10-15 minutes until vegetables are tender.

2 Gradually stir in the potato powder. Remove from heat and stir in the milk. Transfer to a blender or processor and blitz until smooth. Season to taste with pepper and a little grated nutmeg.

3 If necessary, re-heat gently before serving, or chill and serve cold. Swirl 1 tbsp single cream into each serving and garnish with freshly chopped chives.

filling
fish

two 12 4

prawn & potato cakes

- 400g/14oz peeled weight potatoes
- 2 tbsp skimmed milk
- 2 tbsp parsley, finely chopped
- 150g/5oz cooked prawns, defrosted if frozen
- Salt and pepper
- 2 medium slices wholemeal bread, made into crumbs
- Spray oil

1 Boil potatoes. Drain and mash with skimmed milk. Leave until cool enough to handle.

2 Stir in the parsley and prawns and season to taste.

3 Shape the mixture into 4 large cakes about 1 cm/½ inch thick. Place the breadcrumbs on a plate or shallow dish and coat the cakes with the crumbs, pressing them on well.

4 Spray a non-stick pan with sufficient oil to cover the base and cook the cakes over medium heat about 3 minutes. Spray the top of the cakes with oil, turn over and cook a further 3 minutes or until heated through and golden. Serve with No-Check salad.

200g/7oz potato
2 tbsp skimmed milk
Salt and pepper
1 tbsp finely chopped parsley or chives (optional)
1 medium egg, hard boiled
Individual pack Young's Cod Steak in Butter Sauce
30g/1oz frozen peas or petit pois

1 Peel and boil the potato. Drain and mash with the skimmed milk. Season to taste and stir in the herbs, if using.

2 Peel and slice or roughly chop the egg. Microwave or boil the peas.

3 Microwave or boil the fish according to instructions on the pack.

4 Pre-heat the grill.

5 Place the egg in the bottom of a heatproof dish. Top with the peas. Add the fish in sauce, breaking it up gently. Spread the mashed potato over the fish and fork up. Brown under the grill.

6 Serve with additional No-Check vegetables.

115g/4oz smoked mackerel fillets, preferably in strips
1 orange, peeled and segmented
1 tsp chopped fresh mint
Pepper
2 tbsp unsweetened orange juice
2 x 50g/1¾oz wholemeal rolls
No-Check salad to serve

1 Remove skin from mackerel fillets and discard. Cut into about 12 pieces. Place in a shallow dish together with the orange segments. Scatter with the mint. Season with pepper and pour the orange juice over the fish and oranges. Cover and leave to marinate 1 hour.

2 Pre-heat grill to medium.

3 Thread alternate pieces of mackerel and orange onto skewers. (If using bamboo skewers, pre-soak in water about 20 minutes to prevent scorching.)

4 Grill skewers about 4-5 minutes, turning now and again.

5 Serve half to each person with a wholemeal roll and No-Check salad.

salmon & tomato rice

115g/4oz basmati rice
115g/4oz fresh or frozen broccoli
115g/4oz fresh or frozen green beans
2 rounded tbsp frozen peas
400g can chopped tomatoes
180-200g can skinless & boneless pink or medium red
salmon, drained (e.g. Tesco or Glenryk)
Black pepper

1 Boil rice according to instructions on the pack.

2 Boil broccoli, green beans and peas until just tender. Drain and return to pan.

3 Stir in chopped tomatoes and bring to a simmer.

4 Add the salmon, breaking it gently into chunks. Heat through gently. Season with plenty of black pepper.

5 Divide rice and salmon between 2 serving dishes and gently mix together.

pack in the poultry

savoury turkey
& rice

115g/4oz rice
Spray oil
200g/7oz turkey breast meat, cut into small strips
½ red pepper, cut into strips
½ green pepper, cut into strips
115g/4oz mushrooms, sliced
25g sachet Colman's Savoury White Sauce Mix
300ml/½ pint skimmed milk

1 Cook rice according to instructions on pack.

2 Spray a non-stick pan with oil and heat. Sauté the turkey strips over fairly high heat about 3-4 minutes until cooked through. Remove from pan and cover.

3 Add peppers to pan and stir-fry 2-3 minutes until starting to soften. Lower heat, add mushrooms and 1-2 tbsp water to prevent sticking, and cook a further 3 minutes, stirring frequently. Remove pan from heat whilst you make the sauce.

4 Put sauce mix into a small saucepan. Whisk in a little of the milk to make a smooth cream, then gradually whisk in the rest of the milk. Bring to the boil stirring continuously until the sauce thickens, then simmer gently 2 minutes.

5 Add turkey to peppers and mushrooms and heat through. Remove pan from heat and stir in the savoury sauce.

6 Serve half the rice and half the turkey to each person with additional No-Check vegetables.

2 x 100g/3½oz turkey breast steaks/escalopes
30g/1oz half-fat cheddar
2 dspn cranberry sauce
1 medium slice wholemeal bread, made into crumbs
½ tsp dried mixed herbs
Salt and pepper
A little skimmed milk
Spray oil

1 Pre-heat oven to 200°C/gas mark 6.

2 Place the turkey steaks between layers of clingfilm and beat out until very thin. Lay half the cheese at one end of each steak. Top each with 1 dspn cranberry sauce. Fold turkey over and secure with cocktail sticks.

3 Stir the herbs into the crumbs and season with salt and pepper. Dip the turkey into the skimmed milk then coat with the crumbs, pressing them on well.

4 Spray a baking tray with oil. Place the turkey on the tray and spray tops of turkey with oil. Bake approximately 20-25 minutes until turkey is cooked through and crumbs are crisp.

5 Serve either with No-Check salad for a light lunch, or with a jacket potato and No-Check vegetables for a more substantial meal.

Sr

2 mea~   chicken breasts, cubed
100g/3½oz ~.   roccoli florets
1 level tbsp cornflour
225ml/8floz skimmed milk
½ a chicken stock cube (e.g. Knorr)
1 tbsp low-calorie mayonnaise

1 Boil the potatoes. Drain and mash with a little skimmed milk and season to taste. Steam or microwave the broccoli until just tender. Drain.

2 Spray pan with oil and heat. Brown chicken cubes over medium heat about 5 minutes. Transfer chicken and broccoli to an ovenproof dish.

3 Put the cornflour into a saucepan and gradually whisk in the skimmed milk. Crumble in the stock cube. Bring to the boil stirring continuously until the sauce thickens. Remove from heat and stir in the mayonnaise. Stir sauce into the chicken and broccoli.

4 Pre-heat the oven to 200°C/gas mark 6. Spread the mashed potato over the chicken and broccoli mixture and fork up. Cook in pre-heated oven approximately 15 minutes then finish browning under a moderately hot grill.

5 Serve half the pie to each person with additional No-Check vegetables.

pineapple chicken parcels

2 medium skinless chicken breasts
Good pinch of ground ginger
Good pinch of garlic powder
1 spring onion, sliced
4 rings of red pepper
2 rings pineapple canned in juice, drained
2 tsp light soy sauce
85g/3oz rice

1 Pre-heat oven to 180°C/gas mark 4.

2 Cut 2 large squares of foil and place 1 chicken breast on each. Sprinkle the breasts with the ground ginger and garlic powder. Scatter the sliced spring onions over the chicken then top each breast with 2 rings of red pepper and 1 ring of pineapple. Sprinkle each breast with 1 tsp soy sauce.

3 Wrap the foil around each breast into a secure parcel. Place parcels on a baking tray and cook in the pre-heated oven 20-25 minutes, or until chicken is cooked through.

4 Meanwhile boil the rice.

5 Remove the chicken and pineapple from the foil to 2 serving plates. Accompany each serving with half the boiled rice and some mangetout or other No-Check vegetables.

85g/3oz basmati rice
85g/3oz onion, sliced
Spray oil
150ml/¼ pint half-fat evaporated milk (e.g. Carnation Light)
1 tbsp korma curry paste (e.g. Patak's)
2 small skinless chicken breasts
1-2 tbsp skimmed milk (optional)
1 level tbsp dessicated coconut
Salt
2 tsp flaked almonds, lightly toasted
1 tsp finely chopped fresh coriander (optional)

1 Boil the basmati rice according to instructions on the pack.

2 Spray a non-stick frying pan with oil and cook onions gently until soft and golden. Add a little water if necessary to prevent sticking. Transfer to a blender together with the evaporated milk and curry paste. Blitz until smooth. Transfer to a small saucepan.

3 Cut chicken breasts into cubes. Re-spray the frying pan and heat. Add chicken and cook 5-10 minutes, until cooked through, stirring frequently.

4 Meanwhile, heat the sauce over moderate heat 3-5 minutes, stirring continuously. If it becomes too thick, stir in 1-2 tbsp skimmed milk. Stir in dessicated coconut and season to taste.

5 Stir cooked chicken into the sauce and serve sprinkled with toasted flaked almonds.

6 Serve half the rice and half the chicken korma to each person, sprinkled with a little chopped coriander if you like. Accompany with No-Check vegetables, simmered with curry powder and canned tomatoes.

Spray oil
1 small onion, chopped
Salt and pepper
2 x 100g/3½oz thin pork escalopes
150ml/¼ pint chicken stock
Pinch of Italian seasoning or mixed herbs
60g/2oz mozzarella, cut in thin slices
2 tsp finely chopped fresh parsley

1 Spray a non-stick frying pan with oil and heat. Add the onions and cook gently until softened.

2 Season the pork escalopes and add to the pan. Cook 2-3 minutes each side over medium heat. Add the stock and Italian seasoning or mixed herbs and simmer 2 minutes.

3 Place the mozzarella slices on top of the escalopes. Remove the pan from the heat and cover with a lid or foil for 2 minutes to allow the mozzarella to warm and soften.

4 Sprinkle with parsley before serving.

5 Could be served with mashed potatoes, broccoli and green beans or courgettes, or your choice of No-Check vegetables.

Creamy

175g/6oz pork fillet/tender
Spray oil
1 small onion, sliced
4 mushrooms, sliced
1 dspn wholegrain mustard
4 level tbsp half-fat crème fraîche

1 Remove any membrane from the pork and cut into thin slices.

2 Spray pan with oil and heat. Spread the pork over the base of the pan and cook for about 1½-2 minutes each side until cooked through and golden. Remove from pan.

3 Add onion to pan and cook gently until softened. Stir in a tablespoon of water occasionally to prevent sticking Add mushrooms and cook a further 2-3 minutes. Return pork to pan with 1 tbsp water and warm through.

4 Stir in mustard and crème fraîche and heat gently 1 minute.

5 Could be served with rice, pasta or potatoes and No-Check vegetables.

1 tbsp flour
Salt and pepper
500 g/1lb 2oz lean pork cubes
Spray oil
150-175g/5-6oz leeks, washed, trimmed and sliced
1 medium cooking apple, peeled and cut into chunks
½ tsp dried sage
450ml/¾ pint chicken stock

1 Pre-heat oven to 160°C/gas mark 3.

2 Put the flour in a polythene bag and season with salt and pepper. Add the pork and shake to coat.

3 Spray a pan, or casserole that can be used on the hob, with oil and heat. Brown the pork over fairly high heat. Allow pork to brown one side without stirring, then turn pieces over and brown other side. If using a pan, transfer the pork to an ovenproof casserole.

4 Stir in the leeks and apple chunks and sprinkle with sage.

5 Pour over the stock, cover tightly and cook in the pre-heated oven 1½-2 hours until pork is fork tender.

6 Serve quarter of the casserole to each person, perhaps accompanied by boiled or new potatoes and your favourite No-Check vegetables.

115g/4oz Brussels sprouts
Spray oil
2 well-trimmed rashers lean back bacon, chopped
2 spring onions, sliced
2 rings pineapple in juice, roughly chopped
3 tbsp juice from pineapple
200g/7oz boiled new potatoes to serve

1 Trim the stalk end of the sprouts and remove outer leaves. Cut each sprout into 3 or 4 slices. Cook sprouts about 7 minutes in boiling water until just tender. Drain thoroughly.

2 Spray pan with oil and heat. Add the chopped bacon and stir-fry 1 minute.

3 Add the sprouts, spring onions and pineapple to the pan and stir-fry 1 minute.

4 Add the pineapple juice and stir-fry about 2 minutes more until sprouts are tinged with colour.

5 Serve with new potatoes.

two

10 6 sausage, pepper
& new potato pan-fry

4 Wall's Lean Recipe Sausages (or similar very low-fat
sausages around 70 calories each)
Spray oil
1 onion, sliced
175g/6oz frozen mixed peppers
300g/10oz new potatoes, boiled in skins
½ tsp chilli powder (optional)
Salt and pepper

1 Grill sausages, then cut into thick slices.

2 Spray a large non-stick frying pan with oil and heat.
Cook onions and pepper together about 5-7 minutes,
stirring frequently. Remove from pan.

3 Slice boiled new potatoes thickly. Re-spray pan and
heat. Arrange slices over the base of the pan and
allow to brown. Turn slices over and brown other side.

4 Add sausage slices and cooked peppers and onions
to pan. Season to taste with salt and pepper and chilli
powder, if using. Stir 1-2 minutes to heat through.

5 Serve half to each person.

1 tsp oil
1 medium onion, thinly sliced
8 Wall's Lean Recipe Sausages (or similar very low-fat
sausages around 70 calories each)
115g/4oz plain flour
Pinch of salt
1 medium egg
300ml skimmed milk

1 Pre-heat oven to 220°C/gas mark 7.

2 Grease a shallow non-stick tin 23 cm x 30 cm/
9 inches x 12 inches with half the oil. Spread the
onions over the base of the tin and lay the sausages
on top. Smear the sausages with the remaining oil and
roast for 20 minutes.

3 Sift the flour and salt into a bowl, make a well in the
centre and add the egg. Gradually beat milk into the
egg and flour until you have a smooth batter.

4 Remove tin from oven and quickly pour in the batter.
(If your tin is a bit smaller than the recommended size,
use a little less batter.) Return tin to the oven for about
30 minutes until the batter is puffed and golden.

5 Serve one-quarter to each person accompanied by
No-Check vegetables.

mighty
meaty

two   14 ⑧   mint & marmalade glazed lamb with roasted new potatoes

- **400g/14oz new potatoes**
- **Salt and pepper**
- **Spray oil**
- **Good pinch of mixed herbs**
- **2 x 125g/4½oz lamb leg steaks**
- **2 level dspn reduced-sugar marmalade**
- **½ tsp mint sauce**

1 Pre-heat oven to 220°C/gas mark 8.

2 Boil potatoes until tender. Cut in half horizontally and spread out on a baking tray, cut-side up. Season with salt and pepper, spray with oil and sprinkle with mixed herbs. Roast in oven approximately 30 minutes until crisp and golden.

3 Pre-heat grill to high. Season lamb steaks and grill approximately 8-10 minutes each side or until almost done to your liking.

4 Stir the mint sauce into the marmalade and spread over the steaks. Grill 1 minute more.

5 Serve 1 lamb steak to each person with half the roasted new potatoes and your choice of No-Check vegetables.

550g/1lb 4oz well-trimmed weight, shoulder of lamb*
30g/1oz barley
1 litre/1¾ pints boiling water
2 onions, sliced
4 carrots, sliced
2 sticks celery, sliced
1 tsp mixed herbs
2 Oxo lamb cubes
800g/1lb 12oz potatoes, peeled and cut into large chunks
Salt and pepper

1 Cut the well-trimmed lamb into cubes and place in a large saucepan, or casserole suitable for cooking on the hob. Brown the meat for 2-3 minutes. Add the barley and the boiling water. Boil for 2-3 minutes, then remove pan from heat and skim off surface scum with a spoon. Take care – it's hot!

2 Return the pan to the heat and add the onions, carrots, celery, mixed herbs and crumbled stock cubes. Bring to the boil, then cover and simmer very gently 1½ hours, checking and stirring now and again. Add a little more water if you think a lot has evaporated. Add the potatoes, cover and simmer about 45 minutes, or until the meat is tender and potatoes are cooked.

3 Season to taste. Serve each person with quarter of the stew accompanied by additional green No-Check vegetables such as lightly cooked cabbage.

* We bought an 800g boneless, rolled shoulder of lamb and trimmed away about 250g of fat and waste (a total saving of around 1300 calories or 52 Checks!) If buying on the bone, look for one around 900g/2lb.

400g/14oz potatoes
Spray oil
Salt and pepper
1 medium red onion, sliced
250g/9oz lean rump steak, cut into strips across the grain
6 cherry tomatoes, halved
85g/3oz mushrooms, sliced
4 rounded tbsp canned naturally sweet sweetcorn kernels

1 Boil or microwave potatoes in their skins.

2 Pre-heat oven to 220°C/gas mark 8.

3 When potatoes are cool enough to handle, cut into thick wedges. Place on a baking tray, spray with oil, season with a little salt and cook in the top of the oven about 25 minutes or until golden.

4 Spray a non-stick pan with oil and heat. Add the red onion slices and cook gently about 7-10 minutes until softened.

5 Push onions to one side of the pan, turn up the heat to fairly high and add the steak strips. Cook the steak about 2 minutes, searing on all sides. Remove steak from pan. Add the cherry tomatoes and mushrooms to the onions and stir-fry about 2 minutes. Return steak to the pan together with the sweetcorn and heat through 1 minute. Season to taste with salt and pepper.

6 Serve each person with half the steak mixture and half the wedges accompanied by No-Check salad.

note...

If preferred, wedges can be made with sweet potatoes, but this will add 2 Checks (50 cals) per serving.

meatballs in
onion gravy

250g/9oz lean beef mince
250g/9oz lean pork mince
Good pinch white pepper
¼ tsp allspice or mixed spice
1 small onion, grated
1 medium slice bread, crumbed
1 chicken Oxo cube dissolved in 60ml/2fl oz hot water
1 medium egg, lightly beaten
Spray oil
1 medium onion, sliced
3 level dspn Oxo beef gravy granules
300ml/½ pint boiling water

1 Pre-heat oven to 200°C/gas mark 6.

2 Place both types of mince, pepper, spice and grated onion in a bowl. Mix together thoroughly. Mix in the breadcrumbs. Stir in the beaten egg. Stir in the stock and mix thoroughly.

3 Take a heaped teaspoonful of the mixture, shape into a ball about the size of a walnut and place on a large oil-sprayed baking tray. Repeat with remaining mix to make about 24 balls. Place tray in pre-heated oven and cook 20 minutes.

4 Meanwhile, spray a large non-stick pan with oil and cook the sliced onion gently until well coloured. Mix the gravy granules with the boiling water stirring vigorously. Add gravy to onions in the pan (if you think there are any lumps, pour through a sieve). Add meatballs and simmer gently 5 minutes.

5 Serve quarter of the meatballs and gravy to each person. Could be served with mashed potatoes, pasta or rice and No-Check vegetables.

500g/1lb 2oz extra lean (less than 5% fat) beef mince
11g beef stock cube (e.g. Knorr)
2 onions, thickly sliced
3-4 carrots, thickly sliced
1 stick celery, finely sliced (optional)
800g/1lb 12oz potatoes, peeled and cut into large
chunks
900ml/1½ pints hot water
400g can baked beans in tomato sauce
1 dspn Worcestershire sauce, or to taste
Salt and pepper
1 tbsp finely chopped parsley

1 Heat a large non-stick saucepan and cook the mince
until evenly browned. Stir in the crumbled stock cube
and mix well.

2 Stir in the onions, carrots, celery and potatoes, then
pour in the hot water. Bring to the boil, then reduce
heat, cover and simmer about 30 minutes or until
vegetables are tender.

3 Stir in the baked beans and Worcestershire sauce
and heat through. Season to taste.

4 Serve quarter of the recipe to each person sprinkled
with a little chopped parsley.

good
puds

450g/1lb cooking apples
Granulated sweetener to taste
75g/2½oz sugar
2 medium eggs
60g/2oz self-raising flour

1 Pre-heat oven to 190°C/gas mark 5.

2 Peel, core and chop apples. Stew or microwave until just tender. Sweeten to taste with granulated sweetener and transfer to an ovenproof dish that holds about 750ml/1¼ pints.

3 Place sugar and eggs in a bowl and whisk until pale, thick and creamy. Sift flour into the bowl and fold in lightly but thoroughly with a metal spoon.

4 Spread the mixture evenly over the cooked apple and bake towards the top of the oven approximately 25 minutes or until sponge is risen, starting to "crack" and centre is cooked.

250g/9oz red plums
2-3 dspn granulated sweetener
200g pot fat-free natural fromage frais
3-4 drops vanilla extract or essence
2-3 dspn granulated sweetener

1 Cut plums in half, place in a microwavable dish, cover and microwave on high about 2 minutes until plums are soft. Alternatively, stew plums gently in a saucepan.

2 Remove all stones and allow plums to cool completely. Place plums and juice into a blender and blitz just 2-3 seconds. Stir in 2-3 dspn sweetener, or to taste.

3 Mix the fromage frais with the vanilla extract or essence and sweetener to taste. Spoon into the bottom of 2 wine glasses.

4 Spoon the plum purée on top of the fromage frais and chill well before serving.

fruit &
mousse roulade

3 medium eggs
85g/3oz caster sugar
85g/3oz self-raising flour
1 tsp butter
2 small pots diet lemon mousse (e.g. M&S Count On Us
or similar up to 100 calories per pot)
1 kiwi fruit, peeled and thinly sliced

1 Pre-heat oven to 180°C/gas mark 4.

2 Whisk eggs and sugar together until thick and creamy.

3 Sift flour and fold into eggs and sugar.

4 Lightly grease a Swiss roll tin with the butter and pour in the mixture. Bake approximately 15 minutes or until risen and sponge springs back when touched.

5 Invert sponge onto a sheet of baking parchment. Roll up with the paper and allow to cool.

6 When cool, unroll the sponge and baking parchment. Spread with about two-thirds of the mousse and roll up Swiss roll style.

7 Spread remaining mousse on top and garnish with kiwi fruit slices. Best eaten on same day, but will last another day if kept chilled.

8 For a change, try using strawberry mousse and fresh strawberry slices, or chocolate mousse and sliced pears.

1 medium banana, sliced
2 egg whites
50g/1¾oz caster sugar
500ml/half tub of Carte d'Or Vanilla Light ice cream

1 Pre-heat oven to hottest setting.

2 Place the banana slices over the base of an ovenproof plate.

3 Whisk egg whites until standing in peaks. Gradually whisk in sugar and keep whisking until it is thick and marshmallowy.

4 Place the ice cream on the bananas. Spread the egg white mixture all over the ice cream, ensuring it is completely sealed and there are no gaps.

5 Place in a very hot oven and cook 4 minutes until the meringue is tinged with colour.

6 Serve immediately.

350g/12oz mixed dried fruit (nice if a few chopped
glacé cherries are included)
300ml/½ pint hot black tea
350g/12oz self-raising flour
1 heaped tsp mixed spice
1 medium egg, beaten
1 tbsp skimmed milk, if necessary
½ tsp low-fat spread for greasing

1 Place the fruit in a bowl, pour over the hot black tea and leave at least 4 hours or overnight for fruit to plump up.

2 Pre-heat oven to 180°C/gas mark 4.

3 Sift the flour and spice into the fruit and mix well.

4 Add the beaten egg and mix thoroughly. The mixture will seem very dry at first but comes together if mixed well. If necessary, add 1 tbsp skimmed milk.

5 Grease a 1kg/2lb loaf tin, preferably non-stick, with the spread. Pour the mixture into the tin and level off. Bake in the pre-heated oven approximately 1 hour.

6 Turn out onto a wire rack to cool.

7 Wrap in foil or store in an airtight tin. Tastes even better the next day. Slices that are not required immediately can be frozen.